THE BIBLE CURE

FOR

OSTEOPOROSIS

DON COLBERT, M.D.

Living in Health—Body, Mind and Spirit

THE BIBLE CURE FOR OSTEOPOROSIS
by Don Colbert, M.D.
Published by Siloam Press
A part of Strang Communications Company
600 Rinehart Road
Lake Mary, Florida 32746
www.creationhouse.com

Scripture quotations marked NIV are from the Holy Bible, New International Version. Copyright © 1973, 1978, 1984, International Bible Society. Used by permission.

Library of Congress Catalog Card Number:
99-85847

International Standard Book Number:
0-88419-681-X

This book is not intended to provide medical advice or to take the place of medical advice and treatment from your personal physician. Readers are advised to consult their own doctors or other qualified health professionals regarding the treatment of their medical problems. Neither the publisher nor the author takes any responsibility for any possible consequences from any treatment, action or application of medicine, supplement, herb or preparation to any person reading or following the information in this book. If readers are taking prescription medications, they should consult with their physicians and not take themselves off of medicines to start supplementation without the proper supervision of a physician.

0 1 2 3 4 5 6 VERSA 8 7 6 5 4 3
Printed in the United States of America

Strong, Powerful Bones and a Brand-New You!

The Bible says that God is in the business of protecting your bones! Does that sound odd to you? Well, Psalm 34 says precisely that: "Many are the afflictions of the righteous, but the LORD delivers him out of them all. He guards [protects] all of his bones; not one of them is broken" (vv. 19–20, NKJV).

God never intended for you to experience the pain of bone degeneration from osteoporosis or to suffer from a single break or fracture. In fact, this little booklet contains a powerful plan to help you overcome this painful, degenerative process.

Through His divine wisdom, God has provided foods and powerful substances that will help prevent or stop the progress of osteoporosis in your body. In addition, He has blessed you with the power of faith to overcome the challenges that assault your body and your mind. This Bible Cure booklet is designed to provide the wisdom to understand how to use both the natural and divine resources that God has made available to you to defeat the threat of osteoporosis in your life— forever!

God does not purpose for you to grow old hurting. In fact, His plan and purpose for your life is ongoing strength and renewal. In the Bible, you can read His blessing for your life:

> Praise the LORD, I tell myself; with my whole heart, I will praise his holy name. Praise the LORD, I tell myself, and never forget the good things he does for me. He forgives all my sins and heals all my diseases. He ransoms me from death and surrounds me with love and tender mercies. He fills my life with good things. My youth is renewed like the eagle's!
>
> —PSALM 103:1–5

Can I Develop Osteoporosis?

Women are particularly susceptible to osteoporosis, which means "porous bones." It is progressive loss of bone mass that leads to decreased bone density. How prevalent is it? Approximately one in four postmenopausal women have been afflicted with it—which is over twenty million people in the U.S. Osteoporosis often results in painful, unnecessary fractures to the spine, fore-arms, hips, shoulders and ribs.

A Bold, New Approach

Throughout this book I will share practical steps you can take to overcome osteoporosis through natural methods of good nutrition, vitamins, sup-plements, lifestyle changes and exercise. I will also provide you with faith-building scriptures and Bible Cure prayers to empower you to over-come osteoporosis spiritually.

I have good news for you: Osteoporosis is not your destined end in old age. With God's grace and wisdom, health and joy await you!

As you read this book, prepare to win the battle against osteoporosis. You will begin to feel better physically, emotionally and spiritually. This Bible Cure booklet is filled with practical steps, hope, encouragement and valuable infor-mation on how to stay fit and develop a healthy lifestyle that reduces your risk of developing osteoporosis later in life. In this book, you will

*uncover God's divine plan of health
for body, soul and spirit
through modern medicine, good nutrition
and the medicinal power
of Scripture and prayer.*

You will discover life-changing and healing scriptures throughout this booklet that will strengthen and encourage you.

As you read, apply and trust God's promises, you will also uncover powerful Bible Cure prayers to help you line up your thoughts and feelings with God's plan of divine health for you—a plan that includes living victoriously. In this Bible Cure booklet, you will be strengthened in the following chapters:

You can confidently take the natural and spiritual steps outlined in this book to walk a steady path without the pain and suffering of osteoporosis. Let's turn now to a deeper understanding of what you face and how to overcome it.

It is my prayer that these practical suggestions for health, nutrition and fitness will bring wholeness to your life—body, soul and spirit. May they deepen your fellowship with God and strengthen your ability to worship and serve Him.

—DON COLBERT, M.D.

A BIBLE CURE PRAYER
FOR YOU

Almighty God, You are my strength. Give me wisdom and knowledge so that I may apply all that I learn in this book and thereby overcome osteoporosis. Thank You for the awesome gift of the temple of my body. Fill me with the joy and confidence to praise You for victory over osteoporosis even when I experience pain. Heal me with Your Word. Guide me in the pathway of Your healing for my life. Amen.

Chapter 1

Wise
Up to Win

According to God's Word, your bones can be so healthy and strong that they actually rejoice! The Bible says, "All my bones shall say, 'Lᴏʀᴅ, who is like You, delivering the poor from him who is too strong for him, yes, the poor and the needy from him who plunders him?'" (Ps. 35:10, ɴᴋᴊᴠ).

Now, it's doubtful that the psalmist was suggesting that a person's bones could actually speak. But he certainly was implying that a person's bones could feel great when God heals them.

The first Bible Cure step for experiencing healing and health for your bones is gaining understanding. The more you understand this disease, the better equipped you will be to defeat it. God does not leave us ignorant or helpless when facing obstacles in life. He has graced us with the knowledge we need to live healthy, vital lives.

As you grow in knowledge and understanding of osteoporosis, this is my prayer for you taken from the Bible: "Dear friend, I am praying that all is well with you and that your body is as healthy as I know your soul is" (3 John 2–3).

You also need to be aware of the many ways God has provided to care for your temple—which is what the Bible calls your body. "Or don't you know that your body is the temple of the Holy Spirit, who lives in you and was given to you by God? You do not belong to yourself, for God bought you with a high price. So you must honor God with your body" (1 Cor. 6:19–20). You see, caring for your body is more important than you may have thought. God wants you to care for your temple so that you can live a happy, joyful and healthy life serving God.

Straight Talk About Osteoporosis

Osteoporosis is occurring in epidemic pro-portions in the U.S. In fact, osteoporosis affects approximately one out of every four postmenopausal women. If you are in this category, read carefully. Your risk is the greatest. Osteoporosis is not at all common in men. It occurs most often in Caucasian and Asian people rather than individuals of African descent.

Over twenty million people in the U.S. have osteoporosis. The bones most commonly affected by this disease include the hips, spine, ribs and forearms.

Warning Signs

Some of the warning signs that indicate a progressed state of osteoporosis include:

A bone fracture. Bone mass in women usually reaches its peak around age thirty-five and then begins to decrease. Between the ages of fifty-five and seventy, a woman will typically lose one-third of her bone mass. Unfortunately, most women do not realize they are losing bone mass since they experience no symptoms. Often a woman will discover she has osteoporosis only after she sustains a rib fracture, a compression fracture of the spine or a fracture of the hip. These fractures are the most common. Approximately one-third of all women will fracture their hips at some time in their lives, and approximately one-sixth of all men will.

As many as one-fifth of those who experience a hip fracture will die as a direct result. Many of those who survive this tragedy will end up confined to a nursing home.

Loss of height. Get your height checked often. If you are a woman, I strongly encourage you to get an annual physical. Be sure your doctor keeps a chart on your height, measured without shoes.

About a year ago, a new patient came to my office who suffered from severe osteoporosis. She was about sixty years old, and she told me she had lost five inches in height in the past five years. Unfortunately, her previous doctor never measured her height. Therefore, she was never checked for osteoporosis. As a result, she developed a severe case of osteoporosis along with compression fractures that caused her to lose five inches.

A dowager's hump. A dowager's hump is an actual hump that develops due to the progressive curvature of the upper back and neck.

Dental problems. Other signs of osteoporosis include periodontal disease and loss of teeth as osteoporosis affects the jawbone.

All of these warning signs indicate advanced osteoporosis. You may be thinking, *Do I have to wait until I am experiencing structural changes*

in my body to find out that I have this disease?
Absolutely not! Watch for the following early
warning signs that can signal trouble before it's
too late.

Early Indicators

Early warning signs of osteoporosis include:

- A slight loss of height
- Generalized aches and pains—especially
  in the back and hip area
- Rounded shoulders

Ignoring these early symptoms can eventually
cause you to develop a dowager's hump, severe
compression fractures with dramatic loss of
height and severe chronic back pain caused by
compression fractures. Compression fractures
can pinch the spinal nerves, creating chronic pain
and eventually causing hip fractures and fractures
of other bones throughout the body.

The following HealthTip lists some major risk
factors that can help to determine whether or not
you are at risk.

Are You at Risk for Osteoporosis?

Major risk factors for osteoporosis in women include:

1. Inactivity
2. Low calcium intake
3. Postmenopause
4. Premature menopause
5. Caucasian (white) or Asian race
6. Smoking history
7. Slenderness and leanness
8. Short stature and small bones
9. Never pregnant
10. Family history of osteoporosis
11. Heavy alcohol use
12. Hyperthyroidism
13. Hyperparathyroidism
14. Long-term use of corticosteroids
15. Long-term use of anticonvulsants
16. Gastric or small bowel resection

If you have any of these risk factors, you should see your physician and ask him to order a Dexascan, a test to determine if you have osteoporosis.

Understanding Bone Loss

Bone loss actually begins to increase after age forty, and it greatly accelerates in postmenopausal women. Like many women, you may have thought that you did not need to worry about osteoporosis until after you have reached menopause. However, menopause is only one factor in the development of this disease.

I recently treated a thirty-four-year old woman with severe osteopenia, the stage right before osteoporosis in which a

> *I pray that from his glorious, unlimited resources he will give you mighty inner strength through his Holy Spirit. And I pray that Christ will be more and more at home in your hearts as you trust in him. May your roots go down deep into the soil of God's marvelous love. And may you have the power to understand, as all God's people should, how wide, how long, how high, and how deep his love really is. May you experience the love of Christ, though it is so great you will never fully understand it. Then you will be filled with the fullness of life and power that comes from God.*
> —EPHESIANS 3:16–19

significant amount of bone loss occurs. Even though she was only thirty-four years old, had plenty of estrogen and was taking calcium supplements, she already had bone loss. So you see, it's critically important that you begin implementing these principles while you are young—if possible—before you have experienced any degree of bone loss. A major key to overcoming the threat of osteoporosis throughout your entire lifetime is prevention.

Get to Know Your Bones

To prevent and overcome osteoporosis, you first need to understand how your bones mature, develop and then begin to lose mass in midlife.

Many people think that once our bones are formed, they remain the same forever. However, our bones are made of living tissue that is continually being renewed throughout our lives.

There are two main types of bone cells: osteoclasts and osteoblasts. The *osteoclasts* are always searching for older bone that needs to be renewed. These cells dissolve the old bone and leave behind very small lesions. The *osteoblasts* then move into these small spaces and produce new bone. Therefore, old bone is being dissolved continuously, and new bone is being formed. This renewal process is called "remodeling." The status of our bones is actually dependent upon the delicate balance of these two processes.

During growth years, new bone formation dominates, and very little bone is reabsorbed into the body. After puberty and until about age thirty-five, the body maintains a good balance of bone formation and bone reabsorption. However, after age thirty-five the process of dissolving the bone becomes increasingly dominant. After forty it actually accelerates, and after menopause, usually around age fifty, it increases even more.

Usually bone mass reaches its peak when a woman is about thirty years old. Between the ages of fifty-five to seventy, women typically experience a 30 to 40 percent loss of bone mass. Most of this bone loss occurs without any symptoms. Such an individual is at risk of developing a fracture, such as a fractured hip or rib. When a fracture actually does occur, osteoporosis is usually well advanced.

Why Do Bones Weaken?

As we age, our bodies (particularly our bones) absorb calcium with less and less efficiency. A child usually absorbs 50 to 70 percent of the calcium from his or her food. However, adults may absorb only about 30 to 50 percent of the calcium in their diets, and older adults absorb even less calcium.

As you grow older, this lack of calcium is the single most important factor contributing to the decrease of bone mass and the increased risk of chronic osteoporosis. To understand osteoporosis, it's important for you to realize how much your body needs this vital nutrient. We will discuss practical steps to helping your body get the calcium it needs a little later on.

The Role of Digestion

After menopause, many women are extremely deficient in hydrochloric acid, which is a stomach acid that aids digestion. Without enough hydrochloric acid in the stomach, calcium carbonate cannot be absorbed efficiently. A woman with a normal amount of hydrochloric acid in her stomach generally absorbs about 22 percent of the calcium in her diet, whereas an individual with a deficiency absorbs only about 4 percent.

> *My life is poured out like water, and all my bones are out of joint. My heart is like wax, melting within me. . . .*
> *O LORD, do not stay away! You are my strength; come quickly to my aid!*
> —PSALM 22:14, 19

Take a Positive Look Ahead

If you are younger or just approaching midlife, your future health is in your hands. Even if you are experiencing some of the symptoms of osteoporosis, you can combat and even reverse them by understanding this disease.

God has a strong, vital future for you as you walk in His wisdom. This Bible Cure plan for living in divine health can strengthen your bones and empower you to serve Him body, soul and spirit.

A Bible Cure Prayer
FOR YOU

Lord, You have revealed the causes of osteoporosis. In You are also the remedies, cures and preventions for this painful disease. Guide and direct me in applying what I have learned and thereby prevent or overcome osteoporosis in my body. Consecrate me body, soul and spirit to walk in divine health. Amen.

A BIBLE CURE PRESCRIPTION

Memorize and say aloud this healing word from God:

> I am suffering and in pain. Rescue me, O God, by your saving power. Then I will praise God's name with singing, and I will honor him with thanksgiving.
>
> —PSALM 69:29–30

Describe what you learned about how osteoporosis develops:

_____

_____

Write a prayer thanking God for revealing this knowledge about preventing osteoporosis to you:

_____

_____

_____

_____

Chapter 2

Power Up
With Nutrition

God has created the foods that you need to strengthen your bones and provide divine health to your body. These foods have existed from the beginning of time. The Bible reveals:

> And God said, "Look! I have given you the seed-bearing plants throughout the earth and all the fruit trees for your food. And I have given all the grasses and other green plants to the animals and birds for their food." And so it was. Then God looked over all he had made, and he saw that it was excellent in every way. This all happened on the sixth day.
>
> —GENESIS 1:29–31

Decide today to eat right so that you will prevent osteoporosis and arrest any traces of this disease in your body. The best foods from God's creation for you to eat are those rich in calcium and magnesium. Let's explore what they are.

Enjoy a Glass of Milk!

If you are a postmenopausal woman, supplementing your diet with calcium will help reduce bone loss. Small amounts of calcium are found in many foods, but this vital substance is found in large quantities in only a few foods. An 8-ounce glass of milk contains about 300 milligrams of calcium. Most other milk products, such as yogurt, cheeses and buttermilk, also contain high amounts of calcium. However, you should choose low-fat dairy products.

Vegetables such as broccoli, cauliflower, peas and beans are high in calcium. In addition, nuts—including Brazil nuts, hazelnuts and almonds—and seeds, such as sunflower seeds, contain high amounts of calcium.

Avoid Foods That Rob You of Calcium

Avoid eating a lot of asparagus, spinach, chard, rhubarb and beet greens, since these are high in oxalic acid, which inhibits calcium absorption.

Do you drink a lot of carbonated beverages and eat a lot of red meat? These foods contain high amounts of phosphorus, which decreases bone calcium. It's no wonder we are experiencing an epidemic of osteoporosis in the U.S., since the consumption of these items is so high. Eating large quantities of red meat will almost certainly cause a loss of calcium from your bones and increase your risk of osteoporosis.

Eat Foods Rich in Vitamin D

Most people drink milk that's been fortified with vitamin D. However, vitamin D milk and dairy foods can cause magnesium absorption to decrease. Without enough magnesium, the active form of vitamin D in the blood is reduced.

Vitamin D is a fat-soluble vitamin. It is found mainly in meat products—especially in fish liver oils. Vitamin D is actually manufactured in our skin as it comes in contact with the sun's ultraviolet rays. Good sources of vitamin D include egg yolks, butter, salmon, mackerel, herring and other meats. Artificial fats, such as olestra, may prevent vitamin D from being absorbed. Also fat-blockers such as chitosan or the new fat-blocking weight-loss drug orlistat (Xenical) may also decrease absorption of vitamin D.

Isn't it interesting that osteoporosis is most commonly found among the major milk-drinking cultures—the U.S. being one the highest? Milk and other dairy products contain only very small amounts of magnesium. Without adequate magnesium, the body only absorbs about 25 percent of the calcium content in the milk. Vitamin D is very important for the transport of calcium from the intestines into the blood. It also decreases the excretion of calcium from the kidneys and helps the bones mineralize.

Children who receive insufficient amounts of vitamin D can develop rickets, which is a disease that causes the legs to become bowed because the bones are undermineralized. For

> *God arms me with strength; he has made my way safe. . . . You have armed me with strength for the battle; you have subdued my enemies under my feet.*
> —Psalm 18:32, 39

the past forty-plus years most doctors have been recommending that two to three large glasses of milk be drunk every day, which contains between 600 and 900 milligrams of calcium. However, in spite of our high intake of milk and milk products, including ice cream, cheese and milk, we still have an epidemic of osteoporosis. Drinking milk is not the best way for your body to get necessary vitamin D. Sunlight and eating foods with vitamin D do not inhibit magnesium absorption as does drinking milk.

A BIBLE CURE HEALTH TIP

Try Tofu

Research at the University of Illinois has preliminary findings to suggest that using soy products high in isoflavones can build bone mass and help keep bones strong. Foods like tofu, tempeh and other soy foods contain natural phytoestrogens, which help fight osteoporosis.

Consider ingesting soy products with at least 90 milligrams of isoflavones. For example, a cup of soymilk has 30 milligrams and a cup of roasted soy nuts has 60 milligrams.[1]

Magnesium-Rich Foods: A Cornucopia of Choices

Magnesium also helps your body to absorb calcium from your diet, and it also helps your bones to retain the calcium. Without enough magnesium, you are much more prone to lose bone more rapidly. Inadequate magnesium intake is very common in the standard American diet.

Foods that are rich in magnesium include:

- Most nuts, seeds and legumes
- Whole grains, such as whole wheat
- Apples, apricots, avocados, bananas, cantaloupe, grapefruit
- Soy products
- Brown rice
- Garlic
- Lemons
- Millet
- Black-eyed peas
- Brewer's yeast
- Figs
- Kelp
- Lima beans
- Peaches
- Salmon

Herbs than contain magnesium include alfalfa, bladderwrack, catnip, cayenne, chamomile, chickweed, dandelion, eyebright, fennel seed, hops, lemongrass, licorice, paprika, parsley, peppermint, raspberry leaf, red clover, sage and yarrow.

Eating a diet that is high in fats, proteins and phosphorus can also decrease your body's magnesium absorption.

Foods that rob your body of magnesium include:

- Caffeine
- Alcohol
- Tea
- Sugar
- Soft drinks
- Rhubarb

- Spinach
- Almonds
- Cocoa

A Path to Healthy Bones: Nutritional Steps for Preventing Osteoporosis

Follow these guidelines to help insure a future free from the affects of osteoporosis:

Pass on excess protein.

Vegetarians have a lower risk of developing osteoporosis as they age. High-protein diets, egg whites, casein in milk and lactoalbumin are all associated with an increase in the elimination of calcium in the urine. Casein and lactalbumin are also found in many protein supplements. As the amount of protein in your diet increases, the amount of calcium eliminated from your body also increases.

High-protein diets, such as the Atkins Diet, are very common in the U.S. Such diets encourage people to eat very large quantities of meat and should be avoided because they can deplete the body of calcium. I believe that the popularity of such diets is contributing to the high incidence of osteoporosis in this country.

Quit carbonated drinks.

If you are like most Americans, you love soft

drinks and consume them regularly. But soft drinks contain high levels of phosphorous. When phosphorous levels in the blood are high, calcium levels tend to decline. Therefore, the body compensates by pulling calcium out of the bones to raise these calcium levels. Do you know why soft drinks contain high levels of phosphates? Because this chemical helps to dissolve the enormous amount of sugar contained in most soda pop varieties.

Shun sugar and caffeine.

Too much sugar and caffeine in your diet can also cause your body to throw off calcium. Coffee shops are springing up around the country, despite the fact that coffee contains more caffeine than most other drinks. Americans are drinking more coffee than ever, which is another reason we are seeing such an epidemic of osteoporosis in America.

Be finicky about fiber.

Be careful when you eat fiber. Too much fiber can inhibit the absorption of calcium from the intestines. Therefore, when you do eat fiber, either increase the amount of calcium you take, or take it between meals and at bedtime to prevent the fiber from binding the calcium and thus preventing its absorption.

Avoid acidic foods.

Avoid highly acidic foods, for they can destroy your bones. The pH value of foods actually measures the level of acidity or alkalinity of fluids in the body. A pH of seven is neutral. Higher than seven is alkaline, and less than seven is acidic. The main fluids of the body include the blood, the saliva and the urine. The pH of each of these fluids can be tested to determine acidity or alkalinity. It is vitally important that blood maintain a fairly constant pH of around 7.4. If it rises by just 0.1 point acidity from 7.4 to 7.3, you would probably go into a seizure and eventually die.

It is so critically important to maintain the blood pH that the body will actually rob from the bones—robbing from Peter to pay Paul—in order to keep the blood pH constant at 7.4.

The pH of your saliva usually indicates the kinds of foods you have eaten. It should be around 6.5. The pH of the stomach is usually very acidic, and measures around 1.5 to 3.5, in order to digest your food. The pH of urine is the best indicator of acidity in body tissues. The ideal pH of the urine should be somewhere between 6.5 and 7.0.

When an individual's urinary pH is less than 6,

acidosis has occurred. This state is present in the majority of Americans. In fact, whenever I check a urinalysis, at least nine out of ten of my patients have a pH of around 5.0. Acidosis simply means that our bodies are producing too many acids. A high-fat, high-sugar and high-protein diet creates significant amounts of acids in our bodies, and this is reflected in our urinary pH. Exercising the muscles to fatigue also creates a buildup of lactic acid, which will also be reflected in an acidic urine pH reading.

You can easily determine your own body's balance by purchasing pH paper at your local pharmacy and periodically checking your own urine. The best time to test your pH is when you get out of bed in the morning. Or you can go to a doctor and have a urinalysis performed.

It is no wonder that we are experiencing an epidemic of osteoporosis when most Americans drink coffee, eat bread, cheese, meats, fats, pasta, potatoes and other acid-producing foods, while avoiding fruits and vegetables, which are alkaline-producing foods.

Acidosis actually destroys a person's bones by causing minerals to be extracted from them to buffer acids, thus raising the pH of the body.

Before the body actually extracts calcium and other minerals from the bones, it will first attempt to buffer the acids through rapid breathing, which allows the body to rid itself of the carbon dioxide that causes a buildup of acids.

Your body also uses alkaline amino acids to buffer acids. The kidneys will produce bicarbonates that also buffer acids. Finally, if your body is being overwhelmed by acids that the above mechanisms cannot control, it will actually begin to cannibalize your bones, pulling out phosphates, calcium, magnesium, potassium and other minerals in an emergency attempt to buffer the acids.

> *You say, "Food is for the stomach, and the stomach is for food." This is true, though someday God will do away with both of them. But our bodies were not made for sexual immorality. They were made for the Lord, and the Lord cares about our bodies.*
> —1 CORINTHIANS 6:13

In my practice, I see this daily with patients who are taking in significant amounts of coffee, alcohol, proteins, sugars, starches and fats. These individuals are overwhelming their bodies' buffering systems, thereby creating severe acidosis, which cannibalizes their bones.

I remember one lady who was forty years old when she suffered a fractured arm and two fractured ribs after falling while getting out of the bathtub. This lady's diet consisted of large amounts of coffee, soft drinks, sugary foods, high-protein foods and almost no fruits and vegetables. She also smoked and drank a couple of mixed drinks each night.

This diet created such a condition of acidosis in her body that her bones were cannibalized, and a simple fall while getting out of the shower resulted in three broken bones. I immediately sent her over for a Dexascan, a test that revealed severe osteoporosis. I believe it was a direct result of her chronic state of acidosis.

Prefer fruits.

Eat alkaline-producing foods. At least 50 percent of your diet should consist of fruits and vegetables, which are alkaline-producing foods.

Even though lemons, limes, oranges, berries and grapefruit are acidic outside of the body, inside the body they are actually alkalinizing. Alkalinizing foods include any of the following:

FRUIT

Dates	Grapes
Citrus fruits	Apples
Bananas	Cherries
Peaches	Pears
Plums	Papaya
Mangoes	Pineapples
Raspberries	Blackberries
Apricots	Olives
Coconuts	Figs
Raisins	Melons

GRAINS

Millet	Buckwheat
Corn	Sprouted grains

MEAT AND DAIRY PRODUCTS

Nonfat milk

NUTS

Almonds	Brazil nuts

SEEDS

All sprouted seeds

BEANS AND PEAS

Soybeans	Limas

SUGARS

Honey

VEGETABLES

All nonstarchy vegetables

NONTRADITIONAL VEGETABLES

Sea vegetables	Herbs

Chlorophyll foods (wheat grass, barley grass, alfafa, spirulina, chlorella)

Drink lemon water.

In addition, drink one to two glasses of lemon water (add 2 tablespoons of fresh lemon juice to a glass of water) thirty minutes before each meal.

Get green superfood.

And finally, I recommend a high chlorophyll drink such as Divine Health's Green Superfood.[2] High-chlorophyll foods will help to raise the urinary pH and buffer the acids.

Avoid aluminum.

Avoid aluminum in any form since even small amounts can cause extensive bone loss. Aluminum is found in aluminum-containing antacids, aluminum cookware, aluminum cans and aluminum coffeepots.

Osteoporosis American Style

While I was at a conference, a thirty-four-year-old woman asked me if I had any recommendations for osteoporosis other than the prescription medication Fosamax and 1,500 milligrams of calcium a day. This lady seemed much too young to be suffering with such a significant degree of osteoporosis. I questioned her, searching for a possible cause. Her mother didn't have osteoporosis, she appeared to be very healthy, she had eaten a diet with adequate calcium and had exercised.

I continued to question her about her diet, and I learned that she had eaten a very typical American diet: She consumed soft drinks, a lot of meats, starches, salt and sugar. In addition, she ate very few fruits and vegetables. She also drank too much coffee and tea.

Her typical American diet was actually destroying her bones. Her high-protein intake was leaching calcium out of her bones. The salty food she was consuming was robbing her bones as well.

The high-sugar diet, together with the caffeine from the coffee, tea and soft drinks, created an acidic environment in her body.

By eating the standard American diet, many individuals are doing just as this young woman did. They are creating such acidic conditions in their bodies that they are increasing their risk of developing osteoporosis, even at an early age.

Tips for Healthy Eating

Let's review some important suggestions for preventing osteoporosis:

- Let half of your daily diet consist of fresh

fruits and vegetables. This will create an alkaline environment in your body.

- Do not eat a lot of meats, since they tend to form acid in the body.

- Foods that are high in oxalic acid include chocolate, spinach, rhubarb, almonds, cashews, asparagus, beet greens and chard. Therefore, don't take your calcium supplements while eating these foods at the same time. These foods will inhibit the absorption of calcium.

- Whole grains and fiber can also bind calcium. Therefore, it is best not to take calcium or calcium-containing foods at the same time as eating whole grains or fiber.

- Avoid alcohol, coffee, tea, colas and other caffeinated beverages since they create acidity that can leach calcium out of the bones.

- Avoid aluminum in any form.

God's Help

God will give you the wisdom, strength and

determination that you need to plan a diet regime to build up your bones. Focus on the positive steps you can take to prevent osteoporosis, and take this valuable advice from God's Word:

> Do not be wise in your own eyes; fear the LORD and turn away from evil. It will be healing to your body, and refreshment to your bones.
>
> —PROVERBS 3:7–8, NAS

A BIBLE CURE PRAYER
FOR YOU

Almighty God, give me the will power to eat the foods that are best for me and to avoid those foods that rob my body of calcium. Help me to shop for the right calcium-rich foods to strengthen my bones and help prevent osteoporosis. Thank You for creating just the right foods for my body and for giving me the will power to avoid junk foods and fad diets that will harm me. Amen.

A BIBLE CURE PRESCRIPTION

List all the foods and beverages you now consume that you need to avoid in the future.

_____

_____

_____

Now list the foods that you will begin to include in your diet that you have been overlooking:

_____

_____

_____

Write a prayer asking God to guide you when you shop for the foods you need to eat:

_____

_____

_____

_____

Chapter 3

Charge Up
With Exercise

If you have osteoporosis, you may be suffering from painful injuries caused by weak and brittle bones. But I have good news for you. God cares very deeply about you! Everything about you is important to Him, even the strength of your bones. His powerful Word says, "I will seek the lost, bring back the scattered, bind up the broken, and strengthen the sick" (Ezek. 34:16, NAS). God's desire and plan for you includes renewed health and strength.

When you suffer from osteoporosis, you can experience a weakening of your bones as they slowly lose their mineral content and their internal supporting structure. Eventually your bones can become so weak that they fracture easily. Osteoporosis can steal the strength from your bones, leaving you stoop-shouldered and prone to fractures. But there is something you can do to help lower your risk for a break—you can exercise!

Benefiting Bones
With Exercise

Exercise can help prevent osteoporosis, and it can help treat it by providing strength to your bones and muscles. Exercise will slow mineral loss, help you maintain posture and improve your overall fitness, which reduces the risk of falls.

Get Moving!

The sedentary lifestyle common in America is one of the greatest risks for eventually developing osteoporosis. The human bone is a tissue that's changing constantly throughout our lives. It is constantly being remodeled and reformed in response to the demands and stresses that are placed on it by exercise. As old bone cells die off daily, new bone cells are made to replace them.

Weight-bearing exercises will actually stimulate the growth of new bone cells. The bones, however, must be stressed in order to grow. Weight-bearing exercise will not only stop bone loss, but will also increase the mass of bone.

A sedentary lifestyle is death to our bones. As a doctor, I have seen many women develop osteoporosis, and many of these women have had adequate amounts of calcium in their diets. But they don't stress their bones adequately through exercise, and as a result, they lose significant amounts of bone.

Men also lose bone mass as they age, but not to the same degree as women. And is there any wonder this occurs? Most men and women are too tired to go to the gym when they get home from work, so they sit in their recliners and watch TV. They limit their exercise to walking from the recliner to the kitchen and from the kitchen to the bedroom.

> *When I pray, you answer me; you encourage me by giving me the strength I need.*
> —PSALM 138:3

Weight-Bearing Exercises

What exercises will prevent osteoporosis? Many doctors encourage swimming and cycling. However, these exercises will not prevent osteoporosis.

Only weight-bearing exercises will stimulate bone growth. Cycling will stress the leg bones, but it will do nothing to stress the entire skeleton. Swimming puts no stress on the skeleton whatsoever and will not prevent osteoporosis. Aerobic dance, walking or running will stress the leg bones. These activities will not prevent osteoporosis in the spine, arms and so forth.

The only exercises that prevent osteoporosis in the entire skeleton are weight-bearing exercises such as weightlifting and calisthenics. Weightlifters' bones are much thicker than non-weightlifters' bones on the average.

You may decide to join a gym and have a certified personal trainer demonstrate weightlifting exercises that will prevent osteoporosis. In addition, you can buy dumbbells at a department store and begin a basic weightlifting program. Performing calisthenics such as pushups, lunges, squats, seated dips or even lifting up a five-pound bag of sugar, a can of paint or a gallon of bottled water over your head will stress all the major bones in your body and thus stimulate bone growth.

Getting Started

It's very important to know which exercises will

benefit you and which ones you as an individual need to avoid. Never begin an exercise program if you already have osteoporosis without checking with your doctor first. Your doctor will help you tailor an exercise program to your specific needs.

So, Let's Go!

If you've checked with your doctor, then you can begin doing some of these exercises right away. So, let's go!

Osteoporosis primarily affects the bones of the spine, hips and forearms. Therefore, exercises tailored to prevent further loss to these bones are extremely important. Exercises that strengthen the spine will help to prevent bone loss and the resulting disfigurement of the spine known as a dowager's hump.

Do these exercises approximately three times a week.

Overhead Presses. While seated or standing, simply take a pair of 5- or 10-pound dumbbells and lift them over your head five to ten times. Repeat this for two to three sets.

Lunges and squats are simple exercises that will help to prevent bone loss from the hips.

Lunges. To perform lunges, simply place the dumbbells down by your side and step forward with one foot and lunge outward. Then come back to a standing position with the feet together. Start with a comfortable number of repetitions, like two or three. Increase the number as you are comfortable, but check with your physician or physical therapist for a recommended number of repetitions.

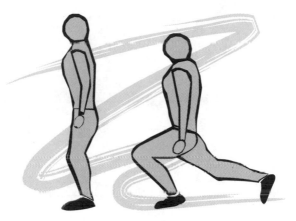

Squats. To perform squats, place the dumb-bells by your side. (You can get larger, heavier dumbbells, such as 20- to 30-pound dumbbells that you hold with two hands.) With legs apart, simply squat down. These exercises are excellent for loading the hip joints, which will help prevent further bone loss. Start with a comfortable number of repetitions, like two or three. Increase the number as you are comfortable, but check with your physician or physical therapist for a recommended number of repetitions.

Pushups. Pushups are great for the forearms. However, many women cannot perform them. I recommend doing pushups from the knees instead of from the feet. Performing these simple exercises will help you to prevent further bone loss. Start with a comfortable number of repetitions like two or three. Increase the number as you are comfortable, but check with your physician or physical therapist for a recommended number of repetitions.

A Final Word About Weight Control

If you have osteoporosis, maintaining your ideal weight can be an important factor. Look up your height and weight in the charts on the following pages and see how close to ideal your weight is. Remember, slenderness and leanness are risk factors for osteoporosis. So do not become too thin or too heavy, but maintain your ideal body weight.

Height and Weight Table for Women

Height	Small Frame	Medium Frame	Large Frame
4'10"	102–111 lbs.	109–121 lbs.	118–131 lbs.
4'11"	103–113 lbs.	111–123 lbs.	120–134 lbs.
5'0"	104–115 lbs.	113–126 lbs.	122–137 lbs.
5'1"	106–118 lbs.	115–129 lbs.	125–140 lbs.
5'2"	108–121 lbs.	118–132 lbs.	128–143 lbs.
5'3"	111–124 lbs.	121–135 lbs.	131–147 lbs.
5'4"	114–127 lbs.	124–138 lbs.	134–151 lbs.
5'5"	117–130 lbs.	127–141 lbs.	137–155 lbs.
5'6"	120–133 lbs.	130–144 lbs.	140–159 lbs.
5'7"	123–136 lbs.	133–147 lbs.	143–163 lbs.
5'8"	126–139 lbs.	136–150 lbs.	146–167 lbs.
5'9"	129–142 lbs.	139–153 lbs.	149–170 lbs.
5'10"	132–145 lbs.	142–156 lbs.	152–173 lbs.
5'11"	135–148 lbs.	145–159 lbs.	155–176 lbs.
6'0"	138–151 lbs.	148–162 lbs.	158–179 lbs.

Height and Weight Table for Men

Height	Small Frame	Medium Frame	Large Frame
5'2"	128–134 lbs.	131–141 lbs.	138–150 lbs
5'3"	130–136 lbs.	133–143 lbs.	140–153 lbs.
5'4"	132–138 lbs.	135–145 lbs.	142–156 lbs.
5'5"	134–140 lbs.	137–148 lbs.	144–160 lbs.
5'6"	136–142 lbs.	139–151 lbs.	146–164 lbs.
5'7"	138–145 lbs.	142–154 lbs.	149–168 lbs.
5'8"	140–148 lbs.	145–157 lbs.	152–172 lbs.
5'9"	142–151 lbs.	148–160 lbs.	155–176 lbs.
5'10"	144–154 lbs.	151–163 lbs.	158–180 lbs.
5'11"	146–157 lbs.	154–166 lbs.	161–184 lbs.
6'0"	149–160 lbs.	157–170 lbs.	164–188 lbs.
6'1"	152–164 lbs.	160–174 lbs.	168–192 lbs.
6'2"	155–168 lbs.	164–178 lbs.	172–197 lbs.
6'3"	158–172 lbs.	167–182 lbs.	176–202 lbs.
6'4"	162–176 lbs.	171–187 lbs.	181–207 lbs.

If you struggle with weight control, no one has to tell you how difficult maintaining your ideal weight can be. But don't despair—God's power can help. Ask Him to help you. He will. The Bible says, "Give all your worries and cares to God, for he cares about what happens to you" (1 Pet. 5:7). Give Him your discouragement, your hopelessness, your sense of defeat and your lack of control. When you blow it, give it all back to Him again. You will be amazed at how much help you will receive. He is a great and wonderful heavenly Father, and nothing is too difficult for Him! (See Jeremiah 32:27.)

Changing the Future

Too many children now lead sedentary lifestyles due to the popularity of sedentary games that they play. When I was young we played football, basketball, baseball and other sports all year round. Today, most children simply play video games and watch TV, doing significantly less physical activity than their parents did years ago. We already have an epidemic of osteoporosis in our country, and most of these people with osteoporosis led fairly active lives in their youth. Think how much greater the epidemic of osteoporosis may be in the future when our children enter their fifties and sixties if they have lived sedentary lifestyles from childhood.

If you have children still at home, help them prevent osteoporosis by maintaining an active lifestyle that avoids destructive habits and foods. A person is never too young to begin to prepare his or her body for a long, prosperous life by following God's Bible Cure plan of exercise, nutrition and positive attitudes.

> *My life is an example to many, because you have been my strength and protection. That is why I can never stop praising you; I declare your glory all day long. And now, in my old age, don't set me aside. Don't abandon me when my strength is failing.*
> —PSALM 71:7–9

A BIBLE CURE PRAYER
FOR YOU

Lord, deliver me from a sendentary lifestyle. Help me to keep my joints limber and my muscles well toned. Show me the level of exercise that is right for me at the present time. Give me the determination to get started and help me maintain the discipline I need to keep going. Thank You for Your wisdom. Amen.

A BIBLE CURE
PRESCRIPTION

List any activity factors that put you at risk for osteoporosis:

_____

_____

_____

List the exercises that you will be committed to doing every day to keep your posture straight and your bones and muscles strong.

_____

_____

_____

Write a prayer to God casting your cares upon Him. End it with a word of thanks.

_____

_____

_____

Chapter 4

Build Up With Vitamins and Supplements

The recipe for turning your health around may include a pound of effort mixed with a pinch of patience. The Word of God says, "It is better to be patient than powerful; it is better to have self-control than to conquer a city" (Prov. 16:32).

Expecting to instantly reverse everything that has been happening in your body may be unrealistic—your body has been torn down over a period of time. However, you can build up your body with wonderful supplements that provide the nutrients you need to battle and win over osteoporosis.

Eating correctly and taking supplements is a long-term process. Be persistent—not impatient. Don't get discouraged if you feel that you are not moving along quickly enough. Start your journey toward feeling better by taking the significant supplements outlined in this chapter.

Significant Supplements

Calcium's effectiveness can be reduced by whole grains containing phytic acid, which may reduce the absorption of calcium and other minerals. It is actually best to take calcium at bedtime, since it is absorbed more readily and can also help you to sleep better.

Stomach hydrochloric acid helps the absorption of calcium tremendously. The first part of the small intestines, called the duodenum, is the main place where it is absorbed.

Calcium is excreted primarily through the intestines, but also through the urine. According to estimates, your body absorbs about 20 to 40 percent of the calcium you take in, and about 40 percent of calcium citrate, but only about 20 percent of calcium carbonate. These are different varieties of supplemental calcium you can buy. Be careful to read the labels to learn what type of calcium you are purchasing.

These rates of calcium absorption can dip down as low as only 5 percent for calcium carbonate if you are a postmenopausal woman who is lacking hydrochloric acid. You could actually be taking in 1,500 milligrams of calcium carbonate a day and only absorbing 75 milligrams, which is only 5 percent. You can see by the loss of calcium daily through non-absorption that taking 1,500 milligrams can still result in significant bone loss.

In addition, I do not recommend some sources of calcium. These include oyster shell, since it may contain significant amounts of lead. Dolomite may also contain relatively high amounts of lead. So, be careful when buying calcium.

A chelated form of calcium, which is bound to an amino acid such as calcium citrate, calcium aspartate or calcium fumarate, is more easily absorbed. Calcium hydroxyapatite, a form of calcium that is derived from bone, is absorbed fairly well. Because it comes from bone meal, it contains all the different minerals in their natural state. However, be careful and don't purchase just any brand, for some can also contain lead. Find a chelated variety at a local health food store. Premenopausal women should take in 1,000 milligrams of chelated calcium a day, and post-menopausal women need 1,500 milligrams a day.

Calcium absorption is dependent upon vitamin D, as well as bile, bile salts and dietary fat. Patients with a low amount of stomach acid (a fairly common occurrence in postmenopausal women) need to take calcium that is already in a soluble state, such as calcium citrate.

Vitamin D is a fat-soluble vitamin found mainly in animals, and especially in fish liver oils. Vitamin D is manufactured in our skin when it comes in contact with the sun's ultraviolet rays. Good sources of vitamin D include egg yolks, butter, salmon, mackerel, herring and other meats. Strict vegetarians who do not eat any meat, eggs or milk products and who do not get adequate sun exposure should take in a multivitamin with at least 400 I.U.s (international units) of vitamin D daily.

> *He renews my strength. He guides me along right paths, bringing honor to his name. Even when I walk through the dark valley of death, I will not be afraid, for you are close beside me. Your rod and your staff protect and comfort me.*
> *—Psalm 23:3-4*

When in Doubt

Are you in doubt about your calcium tablets? You can do your own home test to determine whether the supplement will dissolve readily in your body. Place a tablet in a cup of vinegar and stir it every few minutes. The tablet should be completely dissolved within half an hour. If it isn't, it will not dissolve in your stomach either. If this occurs, choose another variety of supplement.[1]

Magnesium helps to increase the absorption of calcium in your diet, and it also helps your bones to retain or hold on to the calcium.

It is extremely important to supplement your diet on a daily basis with enough magnesium to help prevent osteoporosis. Without adequate amounts of magnesium you are more prone to losing bone more rapidly. The standard American diet provides inadequate amounts of magnesium. Caffeine, sugar, alcohol and soft drinks cause magnesium to be depleted. Magnesium is found naturally in dark green vegetables, nuts, seeds and legumes as well as soy products and whole grains such as whole wheat.

Chlorophyll is the green pigment in plants, and the central atom of the chlorophyll is magnesium. Therefore, high-chlorophyll products are excellent sources of magnesium. Over 60 percent of our magnesium is found in our teeth and bones.

The recommended ratio of calcium to magnesium should be about two to one. In other words, you should take in twice as much calcium as magnesium. Therefore, if you are a premenopausal woman taking 1,000 milligrams of calcium, you should also take 500 milligrams of magnesium. A postmenopausal woman should take 1,500 milligrams of calcium and 750 milligrams of magnesium.

An acidic environment in the stomach is required for magnesium to be adequately absorbed. Eating a diet high in fats, proteins or phosphorus may also hinder magnesium absorption. Similar to calcium, only about 40 percent of the magnesium that we consume is absorbed. Chelated magnesium is the most absorbable form of magnesium such as magnesium aspartate or magnesium citrate. Magnesium salt, such as magnesium oxide

> *For I can do everything with the help of Christ who gives me the strength I need.*
> PHILIPPIANS 4:13

and magnesium carbonate, is not nearly as easily absorbed as chelated varieties.

Vitamins B$_6$, B$_{12}$ and **folic acid** are also important in preventing osteoporosis. Often these vitamins are not present in the foods you eat, so if you do not take a multivitamin every day, you are probably not getting enough. Many times the amino acid homocysteine is elevated in post-menopausal women, which can lead to defective bone formation. Sufficient amounts of B$_6$, B$_{12}$ and folic acid that you need to prevent osteoporosis are usually contained in a standard over-the-counter multivitamin preparation.

Boron is another mineral that is important in preventing osteoporosis because it reduces calcium excretion significantly. Boron is found in apples, pears, leafy green vegetables, nuts and legumes. The recommended dose of boron is 3 to 5 milligrams of boron each day to maintain healthy bones.

Silicon is also important for bone strength. It is found in high amounts in wheat, oat and rice bran. It is also found in alfalfa and in the herb horsetail. Dark green vegetables, avocados, onions and strawberries also contain silicon. This substance helps to restore and strengthen bones by strengthening the connective tissue collagen, which is at the matrix of the bone. Take the supplement as directed on the label.

Natural progesterone is very important in preventing osteoporosis. Natural progesterone can actually increase both bone density and mass. Individuals with osteoporosis who take natural progesterone may notice significant improvements in their Dexascan—which measures bone density and determines the degree of bone loss. I recommend progesterone cream or a natural progesterone capsule. You can find it in most health food stores.

The natural progesterone cream contains 3 percent of this vital substance. Many individuals need a higher percentage, so I routinely write prescriptions for a 10 percent natural progesterone cream. Regular pharmacies don't carry 10 percent cream; however, you can get 3 percent progesterone cream at a health food store. You need to visit a compounding pharmacy in your city, or you can contact the Women's International Pharmacy at 800-279-5708 or at their Internet site, www.wipws.com.

Estrogen is also helpful. I recommend either triple estrogen cream or a triple estrogen capsule, which are natural forms of estrogen that are compounded at pharmacies such as Women's International Pharmacy.

Get a complete medical exam including a gynecological exam, breast exam, mammogram and Pap test before you start taking hormones. Hormone supplements should be added to your nutritional program only under the supervision of your doctor.

Soy contains plant-derived estrogens called phytoestrogens, which are approximately $\frac{1}{100}$ as strong as estrogen. Nevertheless, they do produce a mild estrogen effect. Isoflavone, a primary phytoestrogen, is found in soybeans. One cup of soybeans contains about 300 milligrams of isoflavone, which is roughly equal to one tablet of the estrogen commonly used in hormone replacement therapy known as Premarin. This can help prevent osteoporosis, as well as significantly decrease your risk of developing cancer.

Glucosamine sulfate is very effective in treating osteoarthritis in a dose of 500 milligrams, three times a day. Since osteoarthritis and osteoporosis are usually present at the same time, I place all my patients who have osteoporosis on glucosamine sulfate. Glucosamine sulfate simply provides the joints and cartilage with the raw materials needed in order to repair any damage that's been caused by osteoarthritis.

Ipriflavone was developed from soy iso-flavones, which are phyto-, or plant-derived, estrogens. The ipriflavone, however, does not produce any estrogenic effects. Ipriflavone helps to prevent osteoporosis similarly to how estrogen helps to prevent osteoporosis.

Osteoclasts are bone cells that actually cause the breakdown of the bone. Ipriflavone, however, interferes with their growth, thereby preventing excessive breakdown of bone. It is possible that ipriflavone may not only stop the progression of osteoporosis, but in some cases it may actually reverse it. The dose of ipriflavone that I recommend is approximately 300 milligrams, two times a day.

Osteoporosis Is No Mystery!

It's no mystery why osteoporosis is so prevalent in this country. The average American woman only gets 450 milligrams of calcium a day—nowhere near the 1,000 to 1,500 milligrams that's needed to ward off the disease, says Susan Broy, M.D., director of the Osteoporosis Center at the Advocate Medical Group in Chicago. Ironically, women—who need calcium even more than men do—are more likely to turn away from calcium-rich foods because they're more worried about their waistlines than their bones, Dr. Broy says.

Getting enough calcium is especially important for women approaching menopause, when estrogen levels decline. Estrogen helps bones absorb and keep calcium. When estrogen levels fall, in many cases the bones become weaker. In fact, the highest rate of bone loss occurs in the first five to seven years after menopause. The sad thing about osteoporosis, says Dr. Broy, is that it's often preventable—if you get enough calcium.[2]

HEALTHFACT HEALTHFACT HEALTHFACT HEALTHFACT HEALTHFACT HEALTHFACT HEALTHFACT

It's Up to You

God has created all the substances you need to strengthen your bones and help you to prevent the onset of osteoporosis. Now your part is to use the vitamins and supplements your body needs to build stronger bones and resist disease.

Begin taking the steps you need to supplement your diet, especially with calcium. If you do it now, as you grow older you will enjoy a more active, vital life serving God and celebrating the abundance of good things that He has planned for you.

Jesus said, "My purpose is to give life in all its fullness" (John 10:10). His abundance isn't just for you in your youth, but as you grow older as well.

God plans for the autumn and winter of your life to be fruitful, that is, full of activity, excitement and strength. His powerful Word says, "But the godly

> *But those who wait on the LORD will find new strength. They will fly high on wings like eagles. They will run and not grow weary. They will walk and not faint.*
> —ISAIAH 40:31

will flourish like palm trees and grow strong like the cedars of Lebanon. For they are transplanted into the LORD's own house. They flourish in the courts of our God. Even in old age they will still produce fruit; they will remain vital and green" (Ps. 92:12–14).

A BIBLE CURE PRAYER
FOR YOU

Creator God, thank You for giving wisdom to men to discover and understand the supplements and vitamins I need to help my body prevent and overcome osteoporosis. I thank You that You desire for me to have health and an abundant, full life throughout all of my mature years. Grant me the wisdom to discover what my body needs to grow old both in grace and health. Amen.

R̃ A BIBLE CURE PRESCRIPTION

Check the supplements you need to start using to strengthen your bones:

- ❑ Calcium
- ❑ Magnesium
- ❑ Vitamin D
- ❑ A multivitamin, including B_6, B_{12} and folic acid
- ❑ Boron
- ❑ Silicon
- ❑ Natural progesterone cream

Memorize this encouraging Bible Cure text:

> I love you, LORD; you are my strength. The LORD is my rock, my fortress, and my savior; my God is my rock, in whom I find protection. He is my shield, the strength of my salvation, and my stronghold.
>
> —PSALM 18:1–2

Chapter 5

Look Up
With Dynamic Faith

Have you been told that you have osteoporosis? Believe God for a miracle. He can give you a miracle healing in a minute. I've witnessed such miracles many times, and I have experienced the miracle-working power of God in my own body. But if miracles happened every time we wanted them to happen, they wouldn't be miracles anymore—they would be cures!

Miracles are a divine touch, a moment of supernatural intervention when total healing occurs—but all healing is from God. A doctor can sew up an incision and bind up a wound. But the power that heals the wound and makes you well again always comes from God. I encourage you to pray for a miracle, but don't stop there. Lay hold of the principles of health outlined in this book to aid the healing process. In addition, let's look at osteoporosis in another way that you may not have thought of.

Another Dimension

Throughout this book we have taken a close look at the physical side of osteoporosis. But another dimension exists to this disease that we must also address: a spiritual and emotional dimension.

The Bible strongly suggests that bone disease sometimes has an emotional and spiritual component. Do you know that negative emotions can affect your bones? According to the Bible, they can.

> *A cheerful heart is good medicine, but a broken spirit saps a person's strength.*
> —PROVERBS 17:22

Cheer Up

Proverbs 17:22 says, "A merry heart doeth good like a medicine, but a broken spirit drieth the bones" (KJV). A broken spirit is a spirit that's dejected, and this hurting, depressed spirit will eventually lead to physical and emotional fatigue and a lack of desire to exercise and remain active. Eventually, osteoporosis can result.

God didn't create you to be sad. If you've experienced problems and situations that have robbed you of your joy, turn those circumstances over to God. You'll be amazed at how much He really does love you and how able He is to help you if you let Him. Can you imagine a parent who would want his or her child to be sad instead of happy? Of course not. God is your heavenly Father, and He desires for you to have joy. Why don't you let Him give you His own peace and joy by surrendering your sorrow to Him?

Sadness is only one negative emotion that can affect your bones. Let's look at another.

Persecution
Strikes to the Bone

Have you ever felt persecuted? Perhaps a family member just simply dislikes you. Perhaps someone you thought was a friend has gossiped about you. Perhaps a coworker takes all of the credit for your accomplishments and gives you the blame for his or her failures. Whatever the source, persecution didn't end with the saints of the first-century church. There's plenty of it around today. And believe it or not, the Bible suggests that persecution can also affect your bones.

The psalmist says, "Have mercy on me, O LORD, for I am weak; O LORD, heal me, for my bones are troubled. . . . My eye wastes away because of grief; it grows old because of all my enemies" (Ps. 6:2, 7, NKJV). When David wrote this psalm, he was experiencing so much persecution that his bones were affected.

Psalm 42:9–10 says something similar: "'Why do I go mourning because of the oppression of the enemy?' As with a breaking of my bones, my enemies reproach me, while they say to me all day long, 'Where is your God?'" (NKJV).

Although we no longer commonly use words like "persecution" and "affliction," injustices and personal assaults feel the same to an individual regardless of the generation into which he was born.

We may grin and bear them, but personal attacks, assaults and various forms of injustice strike deeply into our hearts and affect our bodies. The Bible says that when these attacks come often, our bones can be impacted.

God's Word suggests that our physical and emotional well-being is linked together. Environmental stress can take a toll as well.

Less Stress

One significant factor that will rob your body of calcium and make you vulnerable to osteoporosis is stress. Calcium absorption may also be decreased by emotional and physical stress. During times of excessive worry and anxiety, as much as 900 milligrams of calcium a day may be lost in the GI tract.

God's plan is for you to handle stress by casting your cares on Him. "Give all your worries and cares to God, for he cares about what happens to you" (1 Pet. 5:7).

What cares have you neglected to give to God?

- Financial concerns
- Hurting relationships
- Future goals
- Job-related anxieties
- Other: _____

God cares for you and wants to see you through all the stress and worry you may be facing. If you hold on to your stress, then your body will suffer, including your bones! Surrender your cares to Him.

Stress can impact you the same as having a troubled soul.

A Troubled Soul

There is another negative emotion that can lead to bone disease. It is a troubled heart or soul. Have you ever felt deeply troubled? Perhaps it was over something you did or something you witnessed. Hiding such things deep inside can eat away at you and eventually impact your bones. The Bible says, "When I kept silence, my bones waxed old through my roaring all the day long" (Ps. 32:3, KJV).

Such troubling of a person's heart can be caused by a sense of guilt. Make no mistake, guilt is a powerful emotion! Every individual is different. One person may be deeply troubled by something another would scarcely think about twice. That doesn't matter. What does matter is that we keep our hearts clean before God.

> Oh, what joy for those whose rebellion is forgiven, whose sin is put out of sight! Yes, what joy for those whose record the LORD has cleared of sin, whose lives are lived in complete honesty!
>
> —PSALM 32:1–2

If you have trouble in your soul, kneel down and pray in private. Confess all that is troubling you to God. The cleansing you will receive will feel like a breath of fresh, clean air to your soul. None of us were made to carry the weight of guilt around. Jesus Christ died on the cross to rid your life of guilt and sadness forever. He paid the price of sin so that you wouldn't have to. He made a way so that you might live unencumbered and free. He made it so simple.

You can find the answer to every negative emotion in Him.

Breaking the Power of Negative Emotions

You can eliminate negative thoughts and emotions by spiritually feeding on God's Word. Here are some places you can turn to break the power of negative thoughts and emotions in your life:

- Overcoming anger: Ephesians 4:26–27
- Overcoming bitterness: Ephesians 4:31–32
- Overcoming guilt: 1 John 1:9
- Overcoming fear: 2 Timothy 1:7
- Overcoming anxiety: Philippians 4:6–7

Proverbs 14:30 says, "A sound heart is the life of the flesh: but envy the rottenness of the bones" (KJV). However, Proverbs 16:24 says, "Pleasant words are as an honeycomb, sweet to the soul, and health to the bones" (KJV).

You see, a broken spirit, shame and envy can destroy the bones, but pleasant, healing words can build them. If you have osteoporosis, or if you have osteopenia, read the Bible and speak the Word of God aloud. God's Word is full of power and truth. It can change your heart and redirect your emotions.

Accent the Positive!

As you begin to follow the Bible Cure for osteoporosis, you also need to cultivate a positive attitude based on the fruit of God's Spirit so that you can overcome any worry or anxiety that may be paralyzing your efforts. In Galatians 5:21–23 we read, "But when the Holy Spirit controls our lives, he will produce this kind of fruit in us: love, joy, peace, patience, kindness, goodness, faithfulness, gentleness, and self-control." Make the decision now to let these attitudes direct your decisions to win the battle against osteoporosis.

Take These
Bible Cure Steps

Let me suggest that you initiate these spiritual steps to undergird everything you do in the natural to defeat osteoporosis:

1. Reject worry.

Becoming anxious about your future will only serve to weaken you physically and spiritually. Worry never overcame anything. The Bible promises:

> Always be full of joy in the Lord. I say it again—rejoice! . . . Don't worry about anything; instead, pray about everything. Tell God what you need, and thank him for all he has done. If you do this, you will experience God's peace, which is far more wonderful than the human mind can understand. His peace will guard your hearts and minds as you live in Christ Jesus.
>
> —PHILIPPIANS 4:4, 6–7

Replace worry with the confidence and the peace that God's plan for you will overcome osteoporosis.

2. Pray.

Prayer is an unlimited resource for filling your life with God's Spirit, wisdom and strength. He will strengthen your skeletal system and give you the determination to take the natural steps you need to walk in health. Take to heart these encouraging words from the Book of Psalms:

> I love the LORD because he hears and answers my prayers. Because he bends down and listens, I will pray as long as I have breath! Death had its hands around my throat; the terrors of the grave overtook me. I saw only trouble and sorrow. Then I called on the name of the LORD: "Please, LORD, save me!" How kind the LORD is! How good he is! So merciful, this God of ours! The LORD protects those of childlike faith; I was facing death, and then he saved me. Now I can rest again, for the LORD has been so good to me. He has saved me from death, my eyes from tears, my feet from stumbling. And so I walk in the LORD's presence as I live here on earth!

> —PSALM 116:1–9

71

3. Trust in God's Word to heal and sustain you.

Throughout this booklet are scriptures that will strengthen and encourage you. Learn them. Speak them aloud. Let His Word bring guidance and healing into your life.

> Then they cried to the LORD in their trouble, and he saved them from their distress. He sent forth his word and healed them; he rescued them from the grave. Let them give thanks to the LORD for his unfailing love and his wonderful deeds for men.
>
> —PSALM 107:19–21, NIV

A BIBLE-CURE PRAYER
FOR YOU

Heavenly Father, help me to apply all of these things I have learned. I take Your hand for the rest of my journey through the seasons of my life. From fall to winter, I give my life to You. Help me to walk in divine health throughout the path You lay before me and to know You better all along the way. Lord, help me to speak and think positive words so that my life will bring help and refreshing to others. Give me the power to stop destructive habits and attitudes. Fill me with Your joy for life, and give me energy to take the necessary steps to stay fit, both physically and spiritually all of my days. Amen.

A BIBLE CURE PRESCRIPTION

What do you need to overcome in your attitude and outlook on life?

- Bitterness
- Negative thoughts
- Anxiety
- Sadness
- Excessive worry and stress
- Speaking destructive instead of encouraging words
- Other: _____

Check the spiritual steps you have started in overcoming osteoporosis:

❏ I have stopped worrying.
❏ I am praying.
❏ I am learning and applying God's Word.
❏ I am trusting God for health and strength.

Write a prayer thanking God for all the ways He has created to help you overcome osteoporosis in your life:

_____

_____

_____

_____

_____

_____

_____

_____

_____

_____

_____

_____

_____

_____

_____

_____

Begin a Brand-New Life—Today!

God cares about you today, and He cares about your tomorrows. He can see the path that stretches out ahead of you beyond your view. With faith, wisdom, healthy habits and God's wonderful love, I trust He will take you through the autumn of your life, all the way through the winter, with health, vitality, energy and strength.

I encourage you to make a bold commitment to a healthy tomorrow by beginning to implement the Bible Cure plan outlined in this booklet today. Remember, God has provided all that you need for health and healing. He is all you need, so never stop looking to Him.

—DON COLBERT, M.D.

Notes

CHAPTER 2
POWER UP WITH NUTRITION

1. *Doctor's Guide to Medical & Other News,* January 15, 1998, www.pslgroup.com and Selene Yeager, *New Foods for Healing* (Emmaus, PA: Rodale Press, 1998), 397.
2. Donald Colbert, M.D., *Dr. Colbert's Guide to Ultimate Health* (Orlando, FL: Benny Hinn Ministries, 1999), 48.

CHAPTER 4
BUILD UP WITH VITAMINS AND SUPPLEMENTS

1. James F. Balch and Phyllis A. Balch, *Prescription for Nutritional Healing* (Garden City Park, NY: Avery Publishing Group, 1997), 414.
2. Yeager, *New Foods for Healing,* 396.

Don Colbert, M.D., was born in Tupelo, Mississippi. He attended Oral Roberts School of Medicine in Tulsa, Oklahoma, where he received a bachelor of science degree in biology in addition to his degree in medicine. Dr. Colbert completed his internship and residency with Florida Hospital in Orlando, Florida.

If you would like more
information about natural and
divine healing, or information about
Divine Health Nutritional Products®,
you may contact
Dr. Colbert at:

DR. DON COLBERT

1908 Boothe Circle
Longwood, FL 32750
Telephone: 407-331-7007

Dr. Colbert's Web site is
www.drcolbert.com.